CH

THE
BERLIN WALL

THE
BERLIN WALL

BY CHRISTINE ZUCHORA-WALSKE

CONTENT CONSULTANT
A. JAMES MCADAMS
WILLIAM M. SCHOLL PROFESSOR
OF INTERNATIONAL AFFAIRS
UNIVERSITY OF NOTRE DAME

ABDO
Publishing Company

CREDITS

Published by ABDO Publishing Company, PO Box 398166, Minneapolis, MN 55439. Copyright © 2014 by Abdo Consulting Group, Inc. International copyrights reserved in all countries. No part of this book may be reproduced in any form without written permission from the publisher. The Essential Library™ is a trademark and logo of ABDO Publishing Company.

Printed in the United States of America,
North Mankato, Minnesota
102013
012014

Editor: Karen Latchana Kenney
Series Designer: Becky Daum

Photo credits: Lionel Cironneau/AP Images, cover, 2; Schoe/AP Images, 6; AP Images, 9, 16, 19, 30, 34, 36, 68, 77, 78, 80, 83, 88; dpa/picture-alliance/AP Images, 13, 46; Red Line Editorial, 20, 40; zbarchiv/picture-alliance/dpa/AP Images, 26; Bettmann/Corbis, 45, 54, 58, 61, 63, 70; Konrad Giehr/picture-alliance/dpa/AP Images, 48; Dave G. Houser/Corbis, 56; Peter Kneffel/dpa/Corbis, 86; Fabrizio Bensch/Reuters/Corbis, 95

Library of Congress Control Number: 2013946963

Cataloging-in-Publication Data

Zuchora-Walske, Christine.
The Berlin Wall / Christine Zuchora-Walske.
   p. cm. -- (Essential events)
Includes bibliographical references and index.
ISBN 978-1-62403-258-5
1. Berlin Wall, Berlin, Germany, 1961-1989--Juvenile literature. 2. Berlin (Germany)--History, 1945-1990--Juvenile literature. 3. Germany--History--1945-1990--Juvenile literature. 4. Cold War--Juvenile literature. I. Title.
943--dc23

2013946963

CONTENTS

CHAPTER
ONE

ESCAPE FROM EAST BERLIN

It was a hot and sunny day in East Berlin, Germany, on August 18, 1989. Hans-Peter Spitzner was hanging around the city center with his seven-year-old daughter, Peggy.

There was plenty to see in East Berlin, but Spitzner and his daughter were not sightseeing. They had driven the 120 miles (193 km) to East Berlin from Chemnitz, their hometown, for a very special—and dangerous— reason. This reason was so dangerous Peggy did not even know it. Only Spitzner knew why they were really in East Berlin. He was planning an escape.

Two Germanys, Two Berlins

Spitzner was born in 1954. In 1989, he was 35 years old. For his entire life, Germany had been two states—not one country.

East Berliners had to escape through a guarded checkpoint to leave East Berlin.

East Germany was a Communist state. The Soviet Union strongly influenced its politics, economy, and social structure. West Germany, on the other hand, was a capitalist state. Western countries, especially France, the United Kingdom, and the United States, strongly influenced its politics, economy, and society. The Soviet Union and Western countries—and thus East and West Germany—were archrivals.

Likewise, Berlin was two cities, not one. East Berlin, like East Germany, was Communist. West Berlin, like West Germany, was capitalist. The city functioned like an exclave of the state, a West German island completely surrounded by East German territory.

The East Germans had built a border barrier all the way around West Berlin. This barrier consisted of an 11.8-foot (3.6 m) cement wall, electrified and alarm-rigged fencing, barbed wire, armed guards in watchtowers, guard dogs, trenches, tank obstacles, and more. Collectively, this barrier was known as the Berlin Wall.

The Ache to Get Away

The Berlin Wall was not what it seemed. It encircled West Berlin, so it looked as if it was meant to imprison

By 1989, the Berlin Wall had divided the city for all of Spitzner's life.

West Berliners. But West Berlin was not a prison. It was a prosperous and lively city. West Berliners could travel freely to West Germany. And from there, they could go nearly anywhere in the world.

What the Berlin Wall really did was keep East Berliners and East Germans out of West Berlin. East Germany was neither prosperous nor lively. The government controlled most aspects of the economy, from farming to manufacturing. The government also controlled people's personal lives. Citizens did not have the liberty to speak, travel, write, or associate freely. Laws were strict, and spies were everywhere. Goods were scarce and the environment was dirty, making life difficult. Many East Germans wanted out.

Spitzner later explained, "It is hard to describe how life was so hard and dreary. The ache to get away from the . . . secret police snoops, from the grey meat, from the clothes that itched and the air that stung your eyes was palpable."

By 1989, said Spitzner, "My wife Ingrid and I spoke of nothing else."[1]

A Chance to Flee

The Spitzners got their chance in August 1989, when Spitzner's wife, Ingrid, received permission from the East German government to visit her aunt in Austria for her aunt's sixty-fifth birthday. Austria was not a Communist state, so Spitzner's wife was beyond the reach of East German authorities there. They let her go because she was traveling alone. Spitzner and Peggy, left behind in East Germany, could be taken hostage if Ingrid tried staying in Austria longer than she was allowed.

Ingrid had no tricks up her sleeves. The Spitzners had discussed escaping, but she did not know her husband had a specific plan. Spitzner had hidden it from his wife and daughter to protect their innocence in case he failed and they were questioned. Now, with his wife safely in Austria for several days, it was time to act.

On August 16, Spitzner packed two suitcases and drove with Peggy to East Berlin. Members of the US military, many of whom were stationed in West Berlin, often traveled as tourists to East Berlin. And Spitzner had heard they usually were not subjected to vehicle searches. He thought he and Peggy could hide in the trunk of a US military person's car. He hoped he could persuade someone to help them.

For two days, Spitzner approached many US soldiers, worried all the time that the Stasi were watching him. The Stasi were East Germany's secret police, or staff of the Ministry for State Security. They spied on citizens to identify what they called "enemies of the state," people who did not agree with East Germany's Communist government.

Time after time, the Americans refused to help. They felt that Spitzner's plan was too dangerous. If it failed, the American could face criminal charges. Spitzner could go to prison and Peggy to an orphanage.

By August 18, Spitzner had given up. He was in his car with Peggy, ready to leave East Berlin, when he spotted a black Toyota with US license plates. He decided to try one more time.

The car belonged to US serviceman Eric Yaw. Spitzner approached Yaw and explained his idea. Yaw listened and did not say anything for a minute. Fearing the consequences, he had paused to pray for divine guidance. Then he agreed to

TOURISTS

Why would Americans in West Berlin want to visit a dreary, dangerous place such as East Berlin? Most likely, they were just curious. Far away in North America, folks had little chance to see Communism in action. East Berlin welcomed tourists because they brought in foreign money—something the East German government really needed. The government spruced up East Berlin specifically to attract visitors, but those visitors still found it to be a grim place. What they did not know was that outside East Berlin, the rest of East Germany was even more grim.

The Spitzners escaped East Berlin through Checkpoint Charlie.

help. Spitzner and Peggy climbed into Yaw's trunk with their suitcases.

Saved by the Sun

As Yaw drove his car up to a border crossing called Checkpoint Charlie, Spitzner and Peggy huddled silently in the tiny, dark, and stiflingly hot trunk. The car stopped, and Spitzner heard a border guard's boots on the pavement.

His heart sank. He remembered the guards often used infrared scanners to detect body heat, even when they did not physically search a vehicle. He thought the next sound would be the trunk opening.

But that sound never came. Instead, Spitzner heard a shout. The guard was waving Yaw through. "I think being in a black car, which absorbed the heat, saved us," Spitzner later recalled. "The paintwork was already so hot the cameras couldn't detect us!"[2]

Yaw wove left and right around the border barriers, drove a little way, and then stopped. He opened the trunk. "We're in the West," he said. "You can get out now."[3]

CHECKPOINT CHARLIE

Checkpoint Charlie was one of the best-known border crossings between East and West Berlin. It stood between the US sector and the Soviet sector of Berlin. From 1945 to 1990, the city of Berlin consisted of four sectors: British, French, American, and Soviet. The first three made up West Berlin. The Soviet sector was East Berlin.

The sign at Checkpoint Charlie became an international symbol of the Cold War. The Cold War refers to the hostility between Western states (those in North America and Western Europe) and the Soviet bloc (the Soviet Union and the Communist states of Eastern Europe). In English, Russian, French, and German, the sign warned travelers they were leaving the American sector.

Today, the original Checkpoint Charlie sign is preserved in the museum Haus am Checkpoint Charlie. This museum also provides extensive information on the many attempts East Germans made to escape into West Berlin.

The Final Fugitives

Spitzner was elated. He immediately phoned his wife's hotel in Austria, and she got his message just in time. Instead of returning to East Germany, she flew to West Berlin and reunited with her family. All three were now free.

The Spitzners would be the last East Germans to escape through Checkpoint Charlie. They could not have known that a mere three months later, all Germans would be free. On November 9, 1989, the Berlin Wall would come tumbling down in a peaceful, joyous manner that would astonish the whole world.

A REALLY BRAVE THING

On the twentieth anniversary of the Berlin Wall's fall, the three participants in the Spitzners' escape from East Berlin reflected on their experience:

"This was a moment . . . I cannot . . . tell you what I feel."[4] —Hans-Peter Spitzner

"It was a really brave thing to do that for somebody that you have never met before."[5] —Peggy Spitzner

"I would do it again. I would not think twice about it."[6] —Eric Yaw

CHAPTER
TWO

POSTWAR BERLIN

The series of events that led to the Berlin Wall's construction in 1961 began decades earlier. Adolf Hitler and his Nazi political party rose to power in Germany in 1933. Hitler wanted Nazi Germany to take over Eastern Europe and increase its Lebensraum, or living space. He also wanted to purge that space of ethnic groups the Nazis deemed undesirable. In pursuit of that goal, Germany invaded its eastern neighbor, Poland, on September 1, 1939. Thus began World War II.

Almost six years later, World War II was still raging—not only in Europe, but also in Asia and the South Pacific. By April 1945, however, the war was winding down. The United States had developed the world's first nuclear bomb, which would soon end Japan's war efforts. Hitler was hiding out in a bunker underneath Berlin. And Soviet troops were facing approximately 300,000 German soldiers 60 miles (97 km) to the east, ready to mount a final attack against Germany's capital.[1]

US bombers targeted Berlin during an attack on March 6, 1944.

The attack, known as the Battle of Berlin, began on April 16. Hitler committed suicide on April 30. And on May 9, Berlin surrendered, effectively ending the war in Europe. But Berlin's troubles were far from over.

The Potsdam Conference

Before the Battle of Berlin, the Allies had made a plan to meet after the battle and discuss how to manage the borders and governance of postwar Europe. The Allies

STALIN'S BIG HURRY

In spring 1945, Soviet troops approached Berlin from the east as US troops approached from the west. Soviet leader Joseph Stalin desperately wanted the Soviets to capture Berlin first. So he ordered a swift and massive Soviet attack on Berlin. More than 30,000 Soviet soldiers died in this attack, largely because of Stalin's rush.[2]

Why was Stalin so anxious to reach Berlin first? He had already agreed to share postwar control of Germany with the other Allies. Was it for the prestige of landing a final, killing blow to the Nazis? Did he simply mistrust the United States? Both of those reasons may have played a role—and

they are the ones most people believed for decades. But more than 50 years later, British military historian Antony Beever unearthed a Soviet document that revealed the real reason for Stalin's big hurry.

Stalin wanted to capture Germany's nuclear secrets, which were housed at a research center in Berlin. Stalin's spies had informed him of the successful US atomic bomb program. The Soviet nuclear program, by contrast, was struggling. The Soviets found uranium oxide, a mineral that can be made into nuclear fuel, in Berlin. With it, they were able to start building their own nuclear weapon.

Left to right: Prime Minister Winston Churchill, President Harry Truman, and Premier Joseph Stalin at the Potsdam Conference in August 1945

is another name for the Allied powers, which included the Soviet Union, the United Kingdom, France, the United States, China, and dozens of other states. The Allies fought against the Axis powers, which included Germany, Italy, Japan, and several other states.

From July 17 to August 2, 1945, the leaders of the three key Allied powers—Joseph Stalin of the Soviet Union, Winston Churchill of the United Kingdom, and Harry Truman of the United States—met in Potsdam, on the outskirts of Berlin. The main issue they wanted to settle at the Potsdam Conference was how to handle Germany.

The Allies viewed Germany as a major threat to peace and stability in Europe. Germany had played

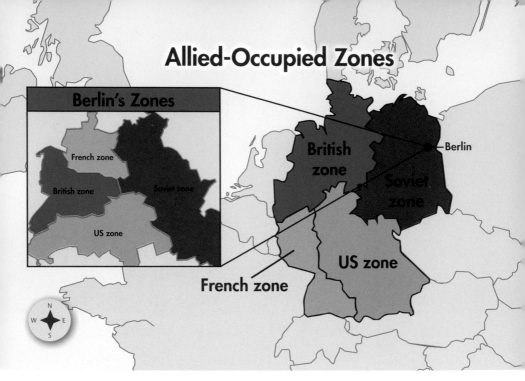

Allied-Occupied Zones

Berlin's Zones

French zone

British zone

Soviet zone

US zone

British zone

Soviet zone

Berlin

US zone

French zone

N
W E
S

a key role in starting World War I (1914–1918) and had single-handedly started World War II. The Allies wanted to disarm Germany and demilitarize its economy and society to discourage it from starting any more wars.

Among many other decisions made at Potsdam, the Allies agreed to share control of Germany through the Allied Control Commission. The commission was made up of four powers occupying Germany: the United States, the United Kingdom, France, and the Soviet Union.

This agreement divided Germany into four zones, each controlled by one of the four states. The British zone covered the northwestern part of Germany. The

Soviet zone lay in the northeast. The US zone was centered south of the British and Soviet zones. These three zones were roughly equal in size. A smaller French zone lay west of the US zone and south of the British zone.

The agreement also divided Berlin into four sectors, similar to the rest of Germany. The Soviet sector included eight districts of eastern Berlin. The French sector comprised two districts of northwestern Berlin. The British sector included four districts of west-central Berlin. And the US sector was made up of six districts in southwestern Berlin.

During talks on transferring power in the zones of Berlin from Soviet to Western troops, negotiators made a critical misstep. They decided that all orders given by the Soviet commander since Berlin had been under Soviet control would stay in force until further notice. This seemed sensible at the time, because the Soviets had secured the city, but it turned into a major barrier to joint governance of the city later on.

Uncooperative Allies

Although the Allies had divided Berlin into sectors of influence, they were supposed to make citywide decisions together. Unfortunately, the Allies could not seem to cooperate now that they had no common enemy in Europe. And the decision about existing Soviet orders complicated matters for the Western Allies. Because the four powers could not get along well enough to make changes by joint decision, the Soviets kept a great deal of control over Berlin. Conflicts of interest among the Allies soon ended their shared governance of the city. The Soviets withdrew from the Allied Control Commission on March 20, 1948.

Despite chronic conflicts among the Allies, for the first few postwar years, Berliners could travel freely between the city's sectors to work and to visit other people. That changed in 1948.

Although the Soviets had the upper hand in governing Berlin, they did not have what they really wanted: complete control of the city. To the Soviets, the Western sectors of Berlin were an unwanted source of foreign influence within the Soviet zone of Germany.

The United States had proposed the Marshall Plan in 1947. The goal of this plan was to improve the economies of European countries with help from US economic aid. On June 23, 1948, the three Western zones of Berlin agreed to use the same currency as part of this plan. The Soviet Union, however, rejected the Marshall Plan, calling it "American economic imperialism."[3]

Stalin responded to the problem of Western influence in Berlin with a simple statement. "Well," he said, "let's try with all our might, and maybe we'll drive them out."[4]

The Berlin Blockade

The Soviets did not actually try to force the Westerners out of Berlin. Instead, the Soviets attempted to make the Westerners so miserable in Berlin they would have no choice but to leave.

On June 24, 1948, the Soviets announced that "technical difficulties" necessitated closing all railways between the Western zones of Germany and the Western sectors of Berlin.[6] Next, they closed the

THE REFUGEE PROBLEM

Another fateful decision made at the Potsdam Conference was an agreement to redraw the borders of Germany, Poland, and the Soviet Union. The Soviet-Polish border moved west, giving an area of Poland to the Soviet Union. The Polish-German border also moved west, giving an area of Germany to Poland.

Poland began deporting its German residents. So did other neighboring states with large German populations. As a result, thousands of refugees began streaming toward Berlin. The population swelled, straining the city's scant resources. During the first postwar year, approximately 12,000 Berliners died of starvation or malnutrition-related sickness.[5]

autobahn (automobile expressway) bridge over the Elbe River just west of Berlin for supposed repairs. Shortly after, they declared all land and water routes into Western Berlin unavailable. As a crowning touch, power stations in Eastern Berlin claimed fuel shortages and stopped supplying electricity to Western Berlin. The largest power station in Western Berlin was nonfunctional because the Soviets had stripped it in 1945. This isolation of Western Berlin became known as the Berlin Blockade. East Berlin also set up a separate city government in November 1948, cementing the city's division.

The Soviets believed a land blockade would drive out the Westerners because they did not think the Allies could supply food and fuel to West Berlin by air. Nazi Germany had attempted a similar airlift during World War II to feed its troops trapped in Stalingrad, Soviet Union, and had failed spectacularly.

The Soviets were wrong. Working together, the Western Allies pulled it off. West Berlin had two airports: one was too small and the other too inconvenient to handle large cargo shipments. So the Western Allies built a bigger, more accessible airfield in the French sector. The United Kingdom and the United

States acquired and transported
the necessary supplies.
Thousands of West Berliners
helped build the airfield and
unload and distribute supplies.
Everyone put up with shortages.

The Berlin Airlift went on
for almost a year, from June 26,
1948, to May 12, 1949. By
April 1949, it was supplying
more than 7,000 short tons
(6,350 metric tons) of supplies
per day. A fully loaded cargo
plane landed in West Berlin
every 62 seconds.[7] The airlift
was a smashing success. It
helped West Berliners survive without falling under
Soviet control. And just as important, it convinced them
for the first time that the Western countries actually
cared about them.

CANDY BOMBER

US pilot Gail Halvorsen met a group of children watching the planes land at West Berlin's Tempelhof Airport. Halvorsen gave them all the chewing gum he had in his pockets. He promised to return the next day.

He collected candy bars and tied them to handkerchief parachutes. The next day, as he landed his plane, he released the candy bombs. Before long, dozens of other pilots, a US candy company, and US schoolchildren were assembling and delivering candy bombs.

CHAPTER
THREE

A STATE DIVIDED

On May 12, 1949, the Soviets lifted the Berlin Blockade—not because they had a change of heart toward the Westerners in Berlin, but because the blockade had backfired. West Berlin was getting along just fine, thanks to the Berlin Airlift. And West Berliners had grown very grateful and loyal toward their protectors.

Relations between the Western Allies and the Soviets continued to deteriorate. On May 23, 11 days after the blockade ended, Germany's Western zones joined to form a new state, the Federal Republic of Germany (FRG), commonly known as West Germany. Its capital was in the city of Bonn. A few months later, on October 7, the Soviet zone of Germany became the German Democratic Republic (GDR), commonly known as East Germany. Its capital was in East Berlin. West Berlin remained a special territory under Allied military supervision.

Berlin citizens read about the lifting of the blockade in the daily newspaper in May 1949.

The two halves of Berlin were still physically connected. Citizens could move about the city freely, and they shared telephone lines, sewage systems, and transportation. But politically and economically, East and West Berlin were growing apart.

The 1950s

Throughout the 1950s, the gap between East and West kept growing. West Germany boomed with rebuilding projects. So did West Berlin, thanks to West Germany and the Western Allies, who contributed money to help West Berlin revive its industries and build a new university. By helping West Berlin survive, Westerners showed their determination to oppose Communism and promote capitalism and democracy. West Berlin prospered.

Meanwhile, East German officials began transforming East Germany into a fully Communist state. They pressured farmers to join government-run collectives. They harassed churches, intellectuals, business owners, and people who lived in East Berlin but worked in West Berlin. In East Germany and East Berlin, food and housing remained scarce. The standard of living declined from 1947 to 1952.

On June 16, 1953, workers in East Berlin went on strike to protest a government-ordered increase in their production quotas. The next day, the protest

COMMUNISM VERSUS CAPITALISM

In a capitalist society, business owners pay workers for their labor. But the business owners own the raw materials, the tools and factories needed to make products, and the products themselves. So the business owners, not the workers, profit most from the workers' labor. The workers cannot even set the price of their labor, because the market determines the price of wages. In a capitalist society, this free market leads to the formation of classes with distinct differences in quality of life.

Communists believe in empowering workers and creating a fairer society. In a Communist society, the government takes control of the economy, land, and production and distribution of goods. This ideal is meant to promote a classless society, where all citizens have a similar quality of life.

Communism offered an alternative system to capitalism and became an international movement in the early 1900s. Much of global politics in the 1900s were driven by competition between the Communist Soviet Union and the capitalist United States. This struggle is known as the Cold War.

German workers threw rocks at Soviet tanks during the June 16–17 strike.

spread to many other East German cities. Soviet troops cracked down harshly over the next ten days, killing several hundred people and injuring more than 1,000 while ending the strike and revolt. Another 1,400 were imprisoned for life.[1]

By 1960, East Germany was in a deep economic recession. It suffered major shortages of food, raw materials for industry, and manufactured goods. In response to the worsening conditions and ongoing harassment, restriction, violence, and harsh demands, East Germans began fleeing west. Walter Kocher, an

East Berlin business owner, was one of them. After the government seized his business, he said, "I no longer had any reason to stay on."[2] By 1961, more than 3 million East Germans had left their homeland.[3] The emigrants were mostly skilled workers, doctors, nurses, teachers, and engineers—people with education and abilities that would enable them to live far better lives in West Germany.

Many of these emigrants left through West Berlin. The long, heavily defended FRG-GDR border was dangerous and difficult to cross. If caught there, a refugee would be arrested and jailed. But West Berlin was fairly easy to enter because the boundaries of West Berlin were not fortified at that time. Once in West Berlin, a refugee could fly to West Germany without interference from East German officials.

East Germany's population—and pool of skilled workers—was plummeting. The East German authorities knew their state had sprung a leak, and they knew exactly where that leak was: West Berlin.

Up Comes the Wall

East German officials responded by increasing their propaganda. They bad-mouthed Westerners, West

MARIENFELDE REFUGEE CENTER

In 1953, West Berlin opened the Marienfelde Refugee Center. It was the first and most important stop for all East German emigrants. The center housed and cared for refugees and shepherded them through the process of getting residence permits for West Berlin and West Germany. At the center, Westerners learned firsthand from refugees about what was happening in East Germany. East German authorities reviled Marienfelde because it supported escapees and gave them a platform for revealing East Germany's weaknesses. Between 1953 and 1990, 1.35 million people passed through Marienfelde.

Berliners, and East German emigrants more than ever. Although they knew people were leaving because Communism was not working, they wanted desperately to believe otherwise—and to convince East German citizens the West was evil. They claimed Westerners were luring Easterners with bribes and even kidnapping them off the streets.

"West Berlin is . . . a big hole in the middle of our republic," said Walter Ulbricht, an East German Communist leader. Through this hole, "trade in people is practised, and . . . food and other materials flow out of our republic."[4] In 1961, the government decided to plug the hole. And it planned to do so quickly and quietly.

Plenty of people had pondered the possibility of a wall around West Berlin. After all, many medieval towns had been walled. And just recently, a wooden wall had been erected in Jerusalem to keep fighting Jews and Arabs apart. But when it came to Berlin, many people dismissed the idea. Berlin was just too big, they thought. It contained large tracts of forest, many rivers and lakes, an intricate sewer system, and extensive railway tunnels. How could all those things be walled off? "It couldn't happen in Berlin," said a West Berlin student. "It just wasn't possible," said West German politician Ernst Lemmer.[5]

Erich Honecker, then East Germany's security secretary, knew it was possible. In fact, he was making it happen right under millions of Berliners' noses. His Soviet and East German superiors had ordered him to seal the border between East Germany and West Berlin, and he was carrying out his assignment skillfully. Surprise was the linchpin of his plan. In mid-July of 1961, Honecker quietly coordinated the stockpiling of materials and gathering of personnel. It appeared like it was a sizeable, but routine, police operation. By the beginning of August, everything and everyone was in place. But even those involved in the preparations had no idea for what they were preparing.

East German soldiers set up barbed wire barriers
to divide Berlin on August 13, 1961.

On the evening of Saturday, August 12, Honecker had orders delivered to the officers in charge of the thousands of police officers and laborers waiting to get to work. Then at midnight, he phoned the army headquarters and barked, "You know the assignment! March!"[6] At 1:00 a.m., the police and workers began sealing the border. Workers barricaded the streets with barbed wire, concrete ramparts, and tank obstacles. Meanwhile, guards stood at 6.6-foot (2 m) intervals all along the border to prevent East Germans from escaping.

Between 5:00 a.m. and 6:00 a.m., East German security officers came out in force. By 6:00 a.m., the temporary barricade was complete. The officers began inspecting and patrolling the streets next to the border, as well as almost all buildings, tunnels, and sewers on those streets. At approximately 8:30 a.m., crowds had gathered on both sides of the border by the crossing points. The West Berliners swarmed right up to the barricade. They were loud and angry, hurling insults at the East German guards and demanding action from their own leaders. The East Berliners were quiet and resigned, and they kept their distance.

RADIO WEST, RADIO EAST

At 4:00 a.m. on August 13, 1961, the station Radio in the American Sector began broadcasting reports about the East German border-sealing operation. Radio Berlin, the East German radio station, did not say a word about the barricade until the afternoon, when it reported citizens saying "they were grateful to be protected from the criminals in the West."[7]

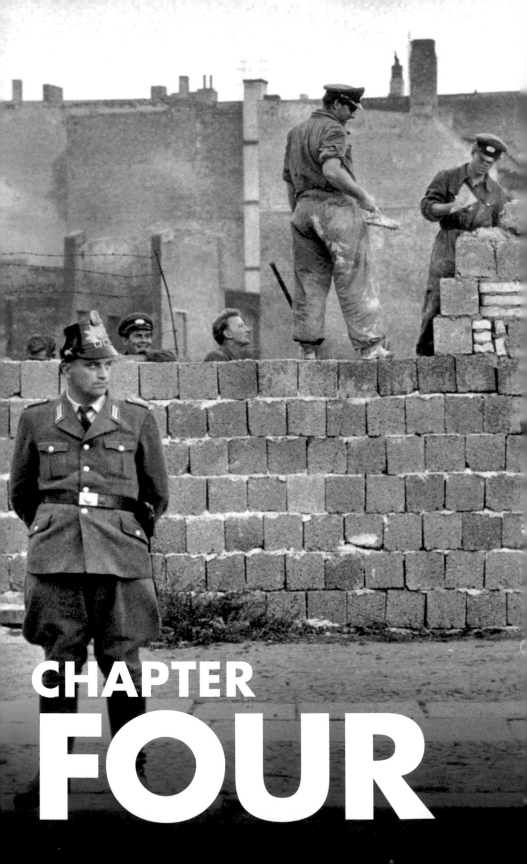

CHAPTER
FOUR

WALL OF SHAME

T he East German government's official newspaper, *Neues Deutschland,* gloated over East Germany's success in building an "anti-Fascist protection barrier."[1] West Germans, meanwhile, called this barrier the *Schandmaur,* or "wall of shame."

Portrait of a Wall

The barrier erected on August 13, 1961, was just the first step in a much grander scheme for barricading East Germany from its neighbors in West Berlin. Workers soon cemented concrete blocks to form a low wall along the political border, with a few deviations around bodies of water. And the fortifications just kept coming. By the time the barrier was complete, it consisted of many layers of security.

Approaching the border from the East German side, the first security layer people encountered was the inner wall. Where buildings already existed, they were at first incorporated into the inner wall. East German workers

East Berlin workers add concrete blocks to the wall on October 7, 1961.

SEVERING INFRASTRUCTURE

The Berlin Wall was not just a multifaceted surface obstacle. The border-sealing project also included cutting telephone lines, tearing up streets, blocking sewers, rerouting water mains, closing off railway stations, and ending all public transportation connections. It hacked the infrastructure of Berlin sharply in two.

bricked up the West-facing windows and doorways of these buildings. Later, these buildings were demolished, and the wall was built up where the buildings once stood. Across open spaces, this inner wall was typically an electrified signal fence that set off an alarm when touched. The inner sides of the wall were painted white so that even at night, guards could easily see a fleeing person. At the foot of the inner wall often lay upward pointing steel spikes meant to discourage or injure fugitives.

The second layer of security consisted of 302 observation towers placed approximately 820 feet (250 m) apart so the guards within them could easily see the entire area between adjacent towers. The guards monitored the strip between the inner and outer walls as well as the neighboring areas of West Berlin and East Germany.

The third security layer included signal devices or watchdogs. These were arranged either in front of or behind the line formed by the observation towers and served a double purpose. They both blocked a fugitive's path and alerted the border guards when someone was trying to flee.

The fourth layer of security was a border patrol road. Patrol and supply vehicles accessed this road through gates in the inner wall. A deep ditch meant to prevent escape by vehicle lined the outer edge of the patrol road.

The fifth security layer was an unmanned area called the control strip. This was a wide strip of sand or fine gravel in which escapees would leave footprints. Tall poles hung with floodlights stood along the line between the ditch and the control strip. The light poles marked the boundary between the manned and unmanned areas. Any border guard who crossed this boundary without permission risked being mistaken for a fugitive.

The sixth and final layer of security was the outer wall. This wall followed the actual political border around West Berlin. It was approximately 11.8 feet (3.6 m) tall and made of concrete slabs topped with a

THE SPIKES

Officially, the spikes at the foot of the inner wall were called "surface obstacles." People referred to the spikes as the "asparagus bed" or "dragons' teeth."[2] Westerners sometimes called them "Stalin's lawn."[3]

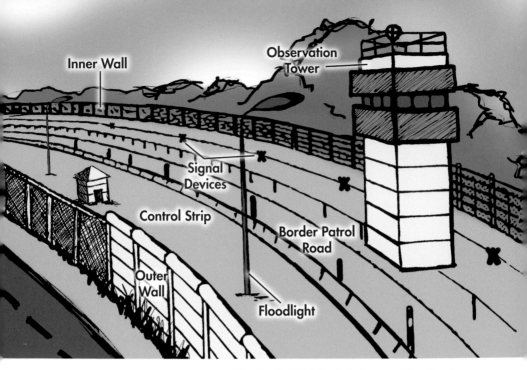

Inner Wall

Observation Tower

Signal Devices

Control Strip

Border Patrol Road

Outer Wall

Floodlight

The Berlin Wall had six layers of fortification.

wide, unscalable concrete tube. The West-facing outer side of this wall is the Berlin Wall so often pictured in Western television broadcasts and news photos. In some places, the outer wall was a wire mesh fence instead.

The total length of the Berlin Wall was approximately 96.3 miles (155 km). Twenty-seven miles (43 km) of the barrier passed through the city center. The other 70 miles (112 km) of the wall encircled the rest of West Berlin.

Early Impacts

The people of West and East Berlin were now completely cut off from one another. Those with friends or family on the other side of the wall could no longer meet. During the wall's initial construction, before the wall grew too tall, people climbed on ladders and platforms to catch glimpses of one another. Many people held up their babies so their loved ones on the other side could get a look.

The wall ran directly through some tightly-knit Berlin neighborhoods. The residents of West Berlin were allowed to stay in these neighborhoods. But those on the eastern side were soon evicted as their government cleared the areas adjacent to the wall. Thus entire communities were torn apart.

Many East Berliners had worked in West Berlin before the wall went up. Jobs there were more plentiful and they paid better. After the wall, these former commuters became unemployed. The East German government put them to work, but usually in menial jobs that paid a fraction of the wages earned in their former positions. They also became subjects of

EVER-EXPANDING WALL

East German authorities constantly expanded, reinforced, and perfected the Berlin Wall. Many sections of the barrier underwent four different versions between 1961 and 1989. The East German government believed the wall demonstrated the country's technological advances.

political harassment and discrimination for having been border crossers.

The situation was even worse for East Berliners who had attended or taught school in West Berlin or West Germany, either by choice or for convenience. These people, according to the East German authorities, had become intellectually tainted. Their educational and career opportunities were severely restricted so

BERNAUER STRASSE

On the 0.6-mile (1 km) east-west *Bernauer Strasse* (Berlin Street), the border ran directly along the base of the apartment buildings on the south side of the street. Those buildings were in East Berlin. The sidewalk, the street, and the buildings on the north side of the street were in West Berlin.

East German officials eventually bricked up, emptied, and then demolished the south-side buildings. But before all that, in mid-August 1961, Bernauer Strasse was the scene of many escapes, attempted escapes, and tragedies. In the first few days, before that section of barrier was constructed, some East Berliners simply walked out the front doors of their homes into West Berlin. Others climbed through windows and lowered themselves to the street via ropes or bedsheets.

As the days ticked by and the barrier strengthened, escape attempts became more dramatic and dangerous. People jumped from upper floors and roofs onto nets and mattresses below, often held by West Berliners. Some of them made it; others missed and died instantly. Some East Berliners, caught while climbing out windows, were grabbed by East German police from above while West Berliners pulled from below. With gravity on their side, the West Berliners usually won these tugs-of-war.

they would not infect others with their corrupted political thinking.

Regine Hildebrandt, an East Berliner who lived near the border, recorded her anguish in the days after the wall went up. "This is a ghastly time in which we live," she wrote. "Our lives have lost their spirit. Nobody enjoys work or life anymore. A petulant feeling of resignation hangs over all of us. There is no point. They will do with us as they like, and we can do nothing to stop them."[4]

Standoff at Checkpoint Charlie

West Berliners, meanwhile, were growing angrier and angrier. They were furious not only at the Communists next door but also at the United States. For several days after the border sealing began on August 13, the US government had not said a word about it, nor tried to help West Berlin.

American journalist Daniel Schorr tried to explain why the US government was doing nothing while the wall went up. "We might have been willing to go to war to defend our right to stay in Berlin," he said, "but can we go to war to defend the right of East Germans to get out of their own country?"[5] The Western Allies were not acting because, technically, their rights were not being infringed.

West Berlin mayor Willy Brandt condemned the wall and begged the United States to show support for West Berlin. He appeared before huge crowds of West Berliners and journalists, urging the Allies to act. He also wrote privately to President John F. Kennedy, asking him to strengthen the US military presence in Berlin.

Kennedy did authorize additional troops for Berlin. The 1,500-man increase, however, was small and symbolic.[6] Scheduled to arrive in late August, the increase was meant not to accomplish a military goal, but to demonstrate the Western Allies had no intention of leaving West Berlin.

The US military continued doing little until October 1961, when East German officials expanded inspections by East German border guards to include spot-checking the identification of Allied civilians entering East Berlin. This violated the Allied four-power procedures agreed upon at the Potsdam Conference. Only Soviet officials had the right to check identification at the entrance to the Soviet sector. The East Germans thought the Westerners would complain about, but not resist, this

West Berlin mayor Willy Brandt, a strong critic of the wall, gives an anticommunist speech on July 19, 1961.

illegal procedure after having already accepted the construction of the wall.

The East Germans were wrong. US general Lucius Clay believed submitting to inspections by East German border guards would destroy morale in West Berlin, not to mention the Allies' legal standing there. With Clay's encouragement, US diplomat E. Allan Lightner Jr. resisted inspection. On the evening of October 22, 1961, Lightner and his wife set off from West Berlin

US soldiers enter East Berlin on October 25, 1961, despite East German refusal to let them enter.

to see a performance at an East Berlin theater. The GDR border guards at Checkpoint Charlie demanded Lightner's identification papers. Lightner refused, demanding in return to see a Soviet official. None were available, and a tense night ensued.

Clay had ordered US troops to be ready for such a situation, and they were. Before long, Lightner had two US infantry squads beside his car. Lightner kept driving a short way into East Berlin, to demonstrate that he could, then turned around and returned to West Berlin.

After this incident, East German border guards persisted in checking Westerners' identification. Many Americans continued resisting. On October 25, Clay sent US tanks to Checkpoint Charlie, where they stood racing their engines. The Soviets responded in kind. For 16 hours, the enemy tanks faced off, mere yards apart. Meanwhile, the world watched in horror. The Soviet Union had recently announced it had a nuclear weapon. This standoff looked as though it could be the beginning of a nuclear war.

Both sides withdrew the next day. President Kennedy had used diplomatic channels to reach an agreement with Soviet leader Nikita Khrushchev. This agreement confirmed Berlin would be divided between the four Allied powers. Citizens of the four Allies could continue to move freely throughout the entire city—but it would not last.

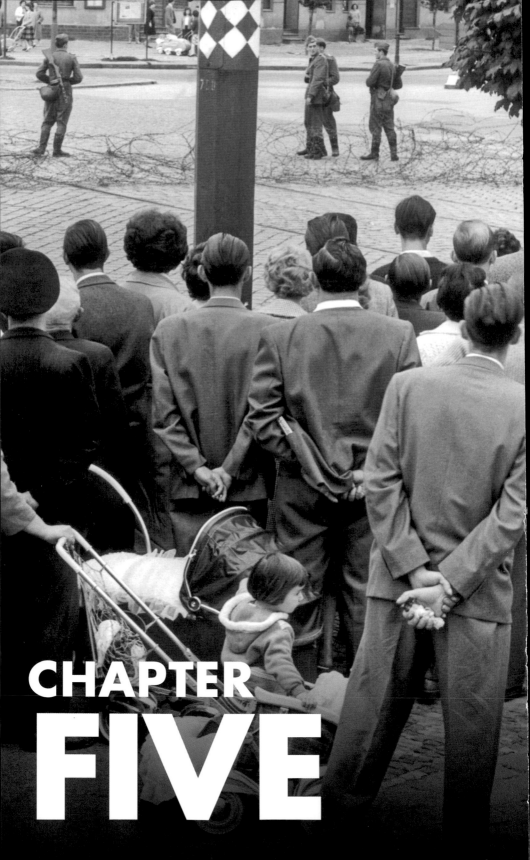

CHAPTER
FIVE

LIFE IN WEST BERLIN

B erliners were limited to their own sectors of the city. West Berliners could make only brief visits to the East for the winter holidays or for situations involving extreme family hardship.

In West Berlin, this restriction created an unusual living environment. West Berliners could travel to West Germany and from there to the world. But doing so was not exactly easy. Driving or taking a train there meant a journey on land through East Germany, with plenty of hassle at checkpoints and the borders. And flying was expensive. Day-to-day life in West Berlin was, for all practical purposes, much like life in a capitalist country. It was just enveloped within a Communist country.

The Economy

Economically, West Berlin could not survive on its own. The GDR-controlled land routes into and out of West Berlin were expensive and unreliable, which complicated manufacturing. And according to the Allied agreements

West Berliners watch armed police standing across the border in East Berlin in August 1961.

made at the Potsdam Conference, West Berlin could not have its own military or manufacture any weapons or equipment with military uses. Furthermore, West Berlin was a city. It had very little farmable land, so agriculture was not a viable contributor to the economy.

From 1961 to 1990, therefore, West Berlin relied on generous help from West Germany. Luckily, West Germany's economy was still booming, and the FRG was deeply committed to West Berlin's

PRESIDENT KENNEDY'S SPEECH

On June 26, 1963, President Kennedy gave a historic speech in West Berlin. In front of a crowd of more than 1 million people, he admired West Berliners' spirit, saying:

Freedom has many difficulties and democracy is not perfect, but we have never had to put a wall up to keep our people in, to prevent them from leaving us. . . . While the wall is the most obvious and vivid demonstration of the failures of the Communist system, for all the world to see, we take no satisfaction in it, for it is . . . an offense against humanity, separating families, dividing husbands and wives and brothers and sisters, and dividing a people who wish to be joined together. . . . Freedom is indivisible, and when one man is enslaved, all are not free. . . . When all are free, then we can look forward to that day when this city will be joined as one and this country and this great Continent of Europe in a peaceful and hopeful globe. . . . All free men, wherever they may live, are citizens of Berlin, and, therefore, as a free man, I take pride in the words Ich bin ein Berliner [I am a Berliner].[1]

survival. One way in which the FRG supported West Berlin was by financing its public infrastructure. West Germany also required certain government departments and production facilities to relocate to West Berlin, providing employment opportunities and services that would not otherwise have existed there. Placing West German government departments in West Berlin also helped West Germany assert control over West Berlin.

Another way in which West Germany helped West Berlin's economy was by offering *Zittergeld*. This was a generous grant paid to people who were willing to stay in or move to West Berlin.

WEST BERLIN'S INDUSTRIES

Although manufacturing was difficult in West Berlin, and it required support from West Germany, it was not impossible. A 2005 declassified US Central Intelligence Agency (CIA) handbook from December 1961 outlined every aspect of life in West Berlin for CIA agents, including economic activity. According to the handbook, approximately 300,000 West Berliners, out of a workforce of 1 million, worked in industry.[2] Its major outputs were electric and electronic products, processed foods, garments, machinery, and motion pictures. Reconstruction of the city was also a major industry.

The Society

Many people had their own reasons for living in West Berlin. Although ambitious young professionals were not interested because the economy was too weak and the city too isolated to boost their careers, West Berlin drew other types of young people for different reasons.

The first big reason was the city's special military-political status. West Berlin was populated by many West Germans, was supported by West Germany, and sent delegates to the West German parliament, but the city was not part of West Germany. Officially, West Berlin remained under Allied occupation. Its FRG parliamentary delegates could not vote. The city could not have defense forces of its own. And a West Berlin residence card excused its owner from the West German draft. That meant West Berlin was the perfect place to avoid an otherwise mandatory stint in the West German military.

The second big reason was the open-minded attitude of most West Berliners. For example, Berlin had a thriving gay and lesbian community. This community had suffered terribly under the Nazi regime but flourished again after 1945. And the freedoms of speech and association were alive and well in West Berlin. Students and other young adults mounted regular political demonstrations for a variety of reasons.

The third big reason West Berlin attracted young people was its vibrant cultural scene. The arts had always been important in Berlin; not even World War II and the Berlin Wall could destroy that heritage. And after 1961, West Germany supported West Berlin's cultural life as strongly as it supported the city's economy. West Berlin had a variety of museums,

STUDENT PROTESTS

Large numbers of students found their way to West Berlin after 1961. They came there not only to avoid the draft and to study—at the Free University, the Technical University, or the Art Academy—but also because they found the city exciting. The open attitudes, cheap rent, and vibrant cultural scene were very appealing to young adults. After their studies were complete, many students stayed on.

These students, former students, and other young adults had a different attitude about German politics than their parents had. In their demonstrations, they loudly opposed the warlike behavior, consumerism, and socially conservative attitudes of both the United States and West Germany.

This hippie party held at the Free University of Berlin in 1967 exemplifies the free spirit of West Berlin.

theaters, and concert halls. Its calendar boasted many music and film festivals. And its nightclubs were open around the clock. Anyone looking for fun did not have to look far in West Berlin.

Relationship with East Berlin

With money pouring in from West Germany and while parties and protests hummed constantly in the background, West Berlin may have seemed to outsiders like a rather self-absorbed city. But West Berliners never forgot their family, friends, and neighbors on the other side of the wall. They supported East Berliners both publicly and secretly. Some West Berliners painted scenes and slogans on their side of the wall. Political rallies and concerts were also staged in front of it. Still others plastered tall billboards with encouragement and news.

West Berliners also reached out to East Berliners over the airwaves. East Berliners could pick up stations including Radio in the American Sector, Radio Free Europe (another US radio station), the British Broadcasting Corporation (from the British sector), and a variety of West German radio and television

Graffiti covers part of the Berlin Wall in 1986.

broadcasts. These broadcasts delivered news that was not filtered or distorted by the Communist government.

Some West Berliners smuggled printed information and consumer goods over the border when they visited East Berlin. If caught, both the smuggler and recipient would be arrested. But it was not as dangerous as another type of smuggling being done by a group of West Berliners. These people were helping East Berliners and East Germans escape.

As soon as the Berlin Wall went up, those trapped on its east side could see the grim future they faced, and many made up their minds to escape it. Just as quickly, an army of helpers formed on the western side of the wall. Most of these helpers were high school and university students.

One particularly effective group of helpers was known as the Girrmann Group. It was named after one of its founders, Detlef Girrmann, an employee of the Free University administration. Its members used a variety of methods, but the most successful were passport forgery or escaping through a route in the sewer system. The Girrmann Group alone helped approximately 5,000 East Germans make it safely to West Berlin.[3]

OTHER HELPERS IN WEST BERLIN

Members of the Girrmann Group were by no means the only escape facilitators in West Berlin. Hundreds of West Berliners, working together and individually, helped friends, family, and perfect strangers across the border. One example is of a young West Berlin woman who made a US Army uniform. Officers gave her buttons and badges when she told them she was making costumes to be used in a play. She then wore her uniform, borrowed a US car and drove to East Berlin, and brought two of her friends back with her. British soldiers also took advantage of a blind spot along a small river between two checkpoints. They hung a rope ladder on the wall to help East Germans swimming to West Berlin.

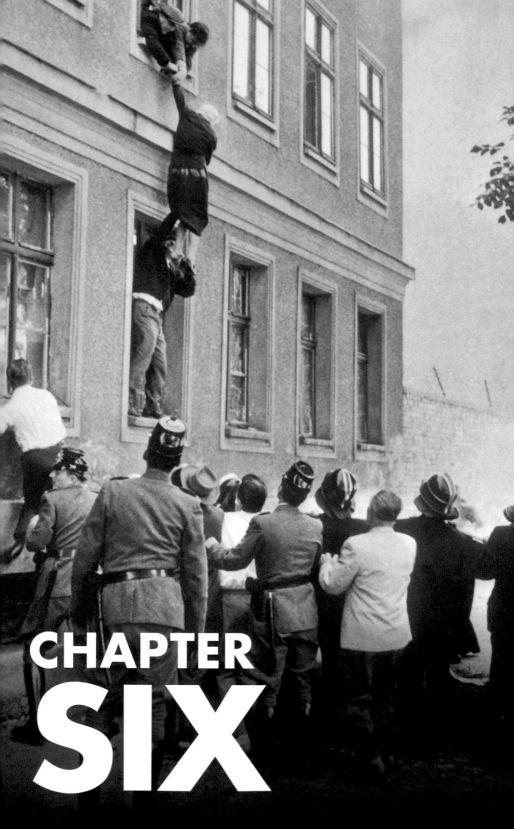

CHAPTER
SIX

LIFE IN EAST BERLIN

Although thousands of East Germans tried to escape to West Berlin, millions never made the attempt. Some East Germans were loyal Communists, but most were just ordinary people resigned to their fate, doing the best they could with their circumstances. While life in East Germany had some socioeconomic benefits, it also had some serious drawbacks.

The Economy

The standard of living in East Berlin was generally better than in the rest of Communist East Germany. This came about for two main reasons. Firstly, East Berlin was a showcase city. The government spent more effort and money there to improve living conditions so East Berlin would not contrast so sharply with the Western sectors. Secondly, East Berlin had a relatively stable economy. It was a manufacturing center, providing approximately 7 percent of East Germany's total industrial output.[1] It produced electric and electronic equipment, turbines,

An East Berlin woman hangs from a window sill as she tries to escape into West Berlin in 1961.

machine tools, high-pressure boilers, antifriction bearings, rubber tires, abrasives, printing equipment, and ready-made clothing not only for East Germany, but also for export to other Communist countries in Eastern Europe.

By the 1970s, GDR government officials in East Berlin were bragging about their "economic miracle."[2] They claimed East Germans had a higher standard of living measured by per-person income than the British did. But the evidence on the ground told another story: the system was not working. Outside East Berlin and a few other showcase cities, East Germany was crumbling. People could rarely buy what they needed or wanted.

WORK ETHIC

In East Germany, as in many Communist countries, the economic system eroded workers' motivation to work diligently. A particular industry was judged a success if it met its production goal, which was set by a governmental five-year plan. Costs were not part of the equation. And if the industry did not meet its goals, it could just tweak the financial numbers to make the outcomes look better. As a result, managers had little reason to require efficiency. East German factories were usually dramatically overstaffed, and workers received many breaks and days off. And because of the larger economy and social safety net, workers did not worry much about losing their jobs or making enough money. In 1993, a union leader in an East Berlin factory looked back on its Communist days and observed, "We have 900 working [on the assembly line] where 2,000 worked before [under Communism]. The 900 produce as much as the 2,000."[3]

Customers wait in line to buy apricots at an
East Berlin fruit stand in 1961.

This was not because they lacked money. They were paid
for their work and prices were low. Rent, for example,
typically cost only 2 percent of one's monthly income.[4]
Rather, it was because food, fuel, and manufactured
goods were constantly in short supply due to the
government's mismanagement.

The Society

While goods were in short supply, work was not hard
to come by. Communists believe in full employment, so
essentially all able-bodied adults had jobs.

THE WAITING GAME

In East Germany, people often stood in shop lines without even knowing what the lines were for, just because there was something to be had. If the something could not be used, it could be traded later for something else useful. Women spent the most time standing in line. This task could take hours, and it might mean leaving work several times per day.

Consumer goods were so scarce that having the money to pay for them and standing in line all day to buy them often was not enough to actually receive the goods. People often had to have connections or influence of some kind in order to persuade shop owners to part with their goods. But the Stasi frowned upon such behavior, so anyone who tried it risked arrest.

Medical care was free, although it was not always of good quality. Young children could attend day care centers and nursery schools at no cost. All education was free, and theoretically, it was available to everybody. But in practice, there were strings attached. If a young person wanted to attend university or get a good job, he or she had little chance of meeting that goal without becoming a member of the Freie Deutsche Jugend (FDJ), or "Free German Youth." The FDJ was a youth organization that was part scouting, part social club, and part political training camp. Military service was also vital to improving one's future.

East Berlin, unlike West Berlin, had no patience for protesting youths. Demonstrating against the government was forbidden.

East German youth groups taught Communist
political ideals to their members.

It would land a person promptly in jail as an enemy of the republic. And simply behaving like a rebellious kid could ruin one's life, too. The GDR cracked down harshly on "hooligans" and "subversives."[5] In the 1960s, hippies were the delinquents of the day. In the 1970s and 1980s, punks were. Many punks were imprisoned for weeks or months in *Jugendwerkhöfe* (youth industrial schools), which were actually super-strict, military-style reeducation camps.

Women experienced far less job discrimination in East Berlin than women in most Western countries did from the 1960s through the 1980s. Many women held important positions, such as judges and doctors. If East German women left work to bear and care for children, they got their old jobs back automatically upon returning to employment. Most women did leave work temporarily for childbearing and child rearing, not only because they wanted to raise families, but because doing so brought financial benefits. Families with children received monetary rewards and housing.

East Germany was serious about stamping out dissent. Every corner of the state—but especially East Berlin, which lay on the enemy's doorstep—was crawling with the Stasi secret police. The Stasi considered themselves the "shield and sword" of the Communist Party.[6] Approximately 274,000 people served in the Stasi between 1950 and 1989. And those were just the official Stasi officers. An additional 500,000 civilians, including children, served as Stasi informants.[7] They monitored every aspect of life in East Germany.

Relationship with West Berlin

Because informants were everywhere and travel was tightly restricted, it was difficult for East Berliners to initiate contact with the West. But they

STASI SNOOPING

The Stasi seemed to stop at almost nothing in their spying efforts. Here are just a few of the ways in which they monitored the East German people:

- They had a telephone system that was mainly used for listening to citizens' conversations.
- They bugged church offices and confessionals with eavesdropping devices.
- They drilled tiny holes in apartment and hotel room walls to film inside the rooms with video cameras.
- Agents lurked and eavesdropped in public bathrooms.

> "Among brothers no one should be better off than the others, and even if he is, for God's sake he should never admit it. . . . Would it be right to remind them that even a jobless guy in Bremen in the West could live better than a skilled worker in Eastern Bitterfeld? Of course, our relatives knew this perfectly well. So . . . we left it alone, drank another beer—and told jokes until dawn. As a child one thing really struck me: in my West/East family, there was a lot of laughter."[8]
> —Claus Christian Malzahn, West Berliner, describing family gatherings in East Germany in the 1970s

could certainly listen to the West, and many did by radio and television in the privacy of their own homes.

The government could not stop the Western broadcasts, so it mounted an effort to stop East Germans from listening instead. In 1961, the government began enlisting the help of FDJ members to influence friends and family members in their circles. Youngsters climbed on roofs and adjusted antennae away from Western signals, lectured their elders on traitorous behavior, and sometimes even reported them to the government.

In 1971, the Allies and the Soviet Union signed the Berlin Agreement. Part of this agreement eased the traffic restrictions to the East. Many Westerners took advantage of the opportunity, and East Berliners welcomed them. Relatives and friends visited—for one day at a time, according to the rules—and rebuilt personal relationships. Everyone had to speak carefully, to avoid trouble for both the travelers and the hosts in case of informants in their midst. But these visits, and the relationships they strengthened, gave people joy and hope.

CHAPTER
SEVEN

CHANGING TIMES

In the late 1970s and 1980s, politics around the world were in a state of upheaval. Erich Honecker, who became the East German leader in 1971, believed strongly in Communism, but many in the country did not have faith in the system. A long series of missteps by Honecker's government, plus the population's growing frustration with the regime, equaled a slowly disintegrating GDR.

The Helsinki Accord

On August 1, 1975, the leaders of all the European countries (except Albania), Canada, the United States, and the Soviet Union signed an international agreement called the Helsinki Accord. Among other things, this agreement made a strong statement about human rights. Countries signing the accord promised to respect "the freedom of thought, conscience, religion or belief, for all without distinction as to race, sex, language or

Erich Honecker's government witnessed the unraveling of East Berlin.

President Gerald Ford, *center*, with Soviet Secretary General Leonid Brezhnev, *left*, and Soviet Foreign Minister Andrei Gromyko, *right*, after signing the Helsinki Accord in 1975

religion."[1] They also promised to promote freedom of movement and reunification of families.

Honecker made a great show of signing the Helsinki Accord as he sat proudly between West Germany's chancellor, Helmut Schmidt, and US President Gerald Ford. But it soon became clear he did not intend to follow through on the promises implied by his signature. In his speech on the occasion, he reminded listeners that the twentieth century's "terrible wars . . . started from the violation of existing frontiers."[2] He went on to say border security was the best way to judge whether a policy really served peace and human interests. In effect, he meant to keep East Germany sealed up tightly.

A handful of East German citizens called attention to the government's dishonesty in 1976. They signed a petition demanding the GDR comply with the Helsinki Accord. They delivered the petition not only to the government, but also to the United Nations and to Western media. The Stasi rounded up many of these people and threw them in jail.

But the petition had started a movement. Before 1976, few people applied for exit visas. Exit visas provided official permission for citizens to leave the country. People applied for different reasons. Some exit visas were for urgent family matters, some were for travels by retired people, and some were for permanent emigration. Regardless of the reason, applying for an exit visa was admitting that one wanted to leave the GDR. This was considered a risky move. But after 1976, the number of applications for exit visas steadily increased. At first, the government cracked down predictably. It approved no visas, and the Stasi intimidated, arrested, interrogated, and imprisoned repeat applicants. Still, the number of applications kept growing into the late 1980s.

Meanwhile, East Germany's economy was in crisis. In the 1980s, the GDR had become dependent on foreign loans. Because its industry was so inefficient and raw materials were so expensive, its state factories could not recoup their costs. The state had to keep borrowing money—mostly from West Germany—in order to stay afloat. Its foreign debt was ballooning, and the GDR had no hope of paying off that debt.

The Gorbachev Effect

In 1985, Mikhail Gorbachev took power in the Soviet Union. Gorbachev was a different sort of leader. He saw Communism was failing, and he preached reform through the ideas of glasnost, or openness, and perestroika, or restructuring. Gorbachev became a catalyst for change in East Germany. But it was not by actively meddling in the GDR's business. Rather, the

Soviet Union began backing away from East Germany. And at critical moments of political upheaval in the Communist bloc of countries, Gorbachev simply looked the other way.

After Gorbachev took power, the Soviet Union started withdrawing the economic help it had provided since 1945. The Soviets had financial problems of their own as a result of the Cold War with the United States. The Soviet Union stopped selling oil cheaply to East Germany. It also stopped holding down prices within Communist Eastern Europe.

HAVES AND HAVE-NOTS

A major factor contributing to the disgust many East German citizens felt for Communism was how much it had failed to live up to leaders' promises. Communism was supposed to fairly distribute resources and give everyone a comfortable life. But in practice, it gave only the politicians comfortable lives.

In East Germany in the 1980s, wages were low and citizens lived in poverty. They put up with constant shortages, restrictions, and bureaucratic red tape. The government could not seem to get anything done. For example, damage from World War II was still unrepaired. Anthony Walske, an American business traveler to East Berlin in the late 1980s, noted that rubble from bombed buildings still lay in heaps, exactly where it had fallen decades earlier. And it seemed to him as though every brick in every standing building throughout the city remained pocked with bullet holes.

Meanwhile, Communist leaders did not suffer from the shortages. The elite had a pampered lifestyle and were hidden from the rest of the state in the countryside near Berlin.

The tide started turning against East Germany in other ways as well. In late 1988 and early 1989, East Germany's neighbors Poland and Hungary both underwent peaceful revolutions, rejecting the strict type of Communism found in East Germany. And on May 2, 1989, Hungary did something even more shocking. It started taking down the fortifications along its border with Austria. Saying the electrified barriers were outdated and too expensive, Hungarian leaders decided they would not continue to maintain them.

Meanwhile, East Germans were becoming bolder. When local elections took place, the government announced the candidates it supported had received 99 percent "yes" votes.

But church observers had witnessed the vote counting, and they knew the announcement was false. They publicly implied the government had committed fraud.

East Germans were disgusted with the rigged election and ongoing travel restrictions. They were also inspired by a free and fair election in Poland and intrigued by what was going on in Hungary. East Germans began streaming out of the GDR. By July, 25,000 of them had headed to Hungary for their summer vacation.[5] This destination was not unusual; Hungary's capital city of Budapest and the nearby Lake Balaton area were favorite vacation spots for Eastern European vacationers. But this summer, the East Germans kept going—right through Budapest, past Lake Balaton, and over Hungary's western border into Austria.

In the old days, events like those happening in Poland and Hungary would have invited swift Soviet military crackdowns. Gorbachev responded differently. In mid-July, he simply declared that all European countries should choose their own sociopolitical systems and forbade the use of military force in this decision-making.

Departures and Demonstrations

In July, August, and September, the number of departing East Germans mushroomed into the hundreds of thousands. Some headed for the Austria-Hungary border. Others sought asylum in West German embassies in Hungary, Poland, and Czechoslovakia, a country made up of modern Slovakia and the Czech Republic.

As East German emigrants traveled onward, Honecker's regime continued ignoring the disaster facing the GDR. Instead of responding to the crisis, they were planning a party for the state's fortieth anniversary on October 7.

October 1989 opened with an eruption of protests. Large demonstrations broke out in the cities of Leipzig, Dresden, Magdeburg, Potsdam, Halle, Karl-Marx-Stadt (now Chemnitz), and elsewhere. These demonstrators demanded freedom of expression, freedom of the press, and freedom to travel.

Honecker instead closed the GDR-Czechoslovakia border and heavily patrolled Poland's border. He also refused to discuss with Gorbachev an East German version of glasnost and perestroika.

East Germans fled across the Hungarian border and into Austria on August 19, 1989, in order to escape to the West.

But the rest of East Germany's Communist Party began realizing the crisis could no longer be ignored. The tension was becoming unbearable.

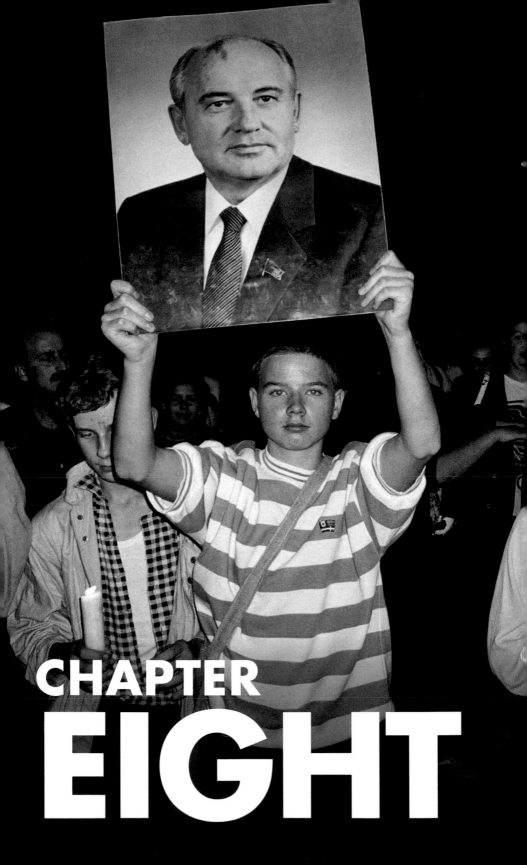

CHAPTER
EIGHT

THE FALL OF THE WALL

After East Germany's anniversary party, the protests kept gaining strength. Communist authorities watched as 70,000 citizens gathered in Leipzig on October 9, 1989. Their discomfort grew on October 16, when the crowd in Leipzig nearly doubled. A throng of 120,000 protesters chanted, "The wall must go!"[1]

Honecker was shocked and angry. He demanded the military use force against the demonstrators. He approved of the way China's Communist government had violently suppressed protesters in Beijing's Tiananmen Square in June. But Honecker stood alone. Although the government had cracked down on earlier demonstrations, many leaders were weary of bloodshed. None of the other high-ranking Communist Party members wanted to use force anymore. Army Chief of Staff Fritz Streletz replied, "We intend to let the whole

Massive protests, such as this one in Leipzig on October 24, 1989, demonstrated the people's displeasure with Communism. The poster shows Soviet leader Mikhail Gorbachev.

Egon Krenz, *left*, shown here with Gorbachev, was perceived as being too close to the Communist Party.

thing take its course peacefully."[2] The next day, the party unanimously voted Honecker out of office.

Three Frustrating Weeks

Then the party voted in Honecker's right-hand man, Egon Krenz. East Germans viewed Krenz with great suspicion. He had been working alongside Honecker for too long. Krenz tried to win over the people with promises of change. But his promises were quickly broken. When the people demanded specific changes, he gave them as little as he possibly could.

The people wanted nothing short of an end to Communism and the right to come and go as they pleased. So when Krenz reopened the GDR-Czechoslovakia border on November 1, many immediately left the country. Over the next week or so, more than 250,000 East Germans fled to Czechoslovakia.[3] The Czech government, unwilling to take responsibility for so many refugees, let the fleeing East Germans pass freely over Czechoslovakia's western border into West Germany.

The East Germans who stayed at home—both citizens and leaders—could see the situation was spiraling into chaos. Day-to-day economic activity had sputtered to a stop. So many citizens had gone there no longer were enough workers left to run the factories, drive the buses, bake the bread, answer the phones, or treat the sick. Millions of protesters gathered in cities all over the GDR. On November 4, more than 500,000 people gathered in East Berlin alone. An equal number gathered in Leipzig on November 6. And the crowds were getting angrier and more confident.

On November 8, the GDR's Communist Party members threw out five high-ranking members leftover from Honecker's regime. Krenz appointed reformers to fill the empty places.

On November 9, the new group of leaders met to assess the state's staggering problems. The economy was imploding, Communism's flaws were being exposed, the people were rising up in anger and leaving in droves. At the same time, Czechoslovakia was threatening to close its border again. Krenz himself was especially worried about the exodus of citizens. He and Party Secretary Günter Schabowski, the East German Communist Party's second in charge, dreamed up what they called a "Christmas present" for the people.[4] They decided to issue new, generous travel regulations. They believed this step would ease the pressure on Czechoslovakia,

Party Secretary Günter Schabowski announced that travel visas would be quickly granted to East Germans during the press conference on November 9, 1989.

convince the people the government truly meant to change, and earn the public's love and praise.

Press Conference

Late that afternoon, Krenz handed Schabowski a press release and the final text of the new regulations as Schabowski headed off to a press conference.

Schabowski was in a hurry, so the two men did not review the regulations together.

Schabowski arrived at the press conference, went over several other items, then announced the new travel regulations. He had not had time to study the text beforehand, so he simply read from the documents Krenz had given him:

> Applications for travel abroad by private individuals can now be made without the previously existing requirements (of demonstrating a need to travel or proving familial relationships). The travel authorizations will be issued within a short time. Grounds for denial will only be applied in particular exceptional cases. The responsible departments of passport and registration control in the People's Police district offices in the GDR are instructed to issue visas for permanent exit without delays and without presentation of the existing requirements for permanent exit.[5]

What the government meant was that East Germans would finally be allowed to travel freely. But in order to do so, they would first have to apply for exit visas, a process that would begin on November 10, after all the border guards, passport officials, and other relevant authorities had been briefed. The visas would be processed promptly, but certainly not instantly. None of these intentions were spelled out explicitly in the documents Schabowski had been given, however.

The room went quiet for a moment. The journalists were not sure what they had just heard, so they started asking questions. Many voices shouted, "When does that go into effect?"[6] Schabowski realized he did not know. He scratched his head, looked through his papers, and whispered to his aides. Then he read aloud from the press release, "*Ab Sofort. Immediately, without delay.*"[7] It was 7:00 p.m., time to shut things down for the night, so he quickly brought the press conference to an end and headed home for dinner.

CLUELESS LEADERS

After Schabowski finished his press conference, the journalists in Berlin were abuzz. But Schabowski clearly had no idea what he had just done. He dismissed everyone matter-of-factly and headed home. The other East German leaders were similarly clueless. They spent the evening at the opera and other entertainment. They were out of touch for hours, not realizing what was happening on the streets of Berlin until the situation had taken on a life of its own.

Upheaval

The journalists had all relayed Schabowski's announcement. But it was not until the Associated Press (AP) released its story that the news really began to spread. The AP wrote, "According to information

Young Germans sing and celebrate atop the
Berlin Wall on November 10, 1989.

supplied by . . . Günter Schabowski, the GDR is
opening its borders."[8]

Soon, other news agencies were picking up
that sentence. When a West German television
news program broadcast it at 8:00 p.m., it started
an upheaval. East Berliners started flocking to the
checkpoints along the wall. They wanted to test what
they had heard by attempting to travel across the border.
The border guards, however, had not yet been briefed on
the new regulations. They did not know what to do.

By 9:20 p.m., approximately 500 to 1,000 East
Berliners had gathered at the Bornholmer Strasse
checkpoint alone.[9] To relieve some of this pressure,
the senior officials there let the pushiest people
through, essentially deporting them. But the people

just kept coming. They came to all the checkpoints, and they came by the thousands. By 11:30 p.m., the crowds at Bornholmer Strasse were so big the checkpoint commander, concerned for the safety of his men, simply threw up the barrier and let people pass through without being checked. Soon all the other checkpoints were opened, too.

East Berliners walked, ran, and practically flew over the border into West Berlin. There, large crowds had already gathered to welcome their neighbors with roses and champagne. The Berliners greeted one another with hugs and exultant shouts. People climbed on top of the Berlin Wall and danced for joy. *Die Mauer ist weg!* they yelled. "The wall is gone!"[10]

PARTY OF THE CENTURY

The party that had broken out in Berlin in the final hours of November 9 went on for days. Checkpoints abandoned all formalities, and people passed freely back and forth between East and West Berlin. West Berliners patted the roofs of the East Berliners' little Trabant automobiles and high-fived the occupants as they streamed over the border. West Berlin banks handed out welcome money, 100 deutsche marks, to the visiting East Berliners. On Kurfürstendamm, West Berlin's main shopping street, many restaurants handed the visitors free drinks. Enormous crowds gathered at the Brandenburg Gate. People hacked at the wall with hammers and other sharp objects—some to play a part in its demise, some for souvenirs, and some just because they could.

CHAPTER NINE

A CHANGING WORLD

The fall of the Berlin Wall was the climax of a world-changing year. Throughout the Soviet bloc, reformers gained power and—using different means in different countries—brought four decades of Communist rule to an end.

The reform movement had begun in Poland in 1980, when a noncommunist trade union called Solidarity had formed. Through sheer determination and against all odds, Solidarity survived until (and beyond) 1989, when Poland's Communist government had grown weak enough to be toppled and replaced.

The reform movement in the Soviet bloc had caught a break in 1985, when Gorbachev came to power. Among many other things, Gorbachev abandoned the policy of his predecessors to intervene with military force when necessary to preserve Communist rule in the region.

The protests in Poland encouraged dissent and change throughout the Soviet bloc in 1989.

Gorbachev encouraged local Communist leaders to find other ways to gain support for their rule.

This policy change had emboldened reformers not only in Poland, but also in Hungary. In Hungary, change came from within the government. Throughout the 1980s, reformers doggedly, quietly worked their way

THE POLISH STORY

After World War II, Poland's economy grew under Communist rule. But so did its people's discontent. When the economy faltered in the late 1970s, Poles began opposing their government.

In 1980, Polish strike leader Lech Walesa led the shipyard workers in Gdansk on strike. They demanded better civil rights, labor reform, and the right to establish a trade union free of Communist control. The workers refused to back down—and eventually got what they wanted in the Gdansk Agreement. Thus, the Solidarity trade union was born. It grew rapidly. Before long, approximately 10 million people had joined.[1] Solidarity became the main vehicle for opposing Communist rule.

From 1981 to 1983, Communist authorities imposed martial law to strengthen their failing grip on Poland. The army and special police units seized control of the country, arrested Solidarity leaders, and outlawed union activity. But union members kept operating secretly—even in jail. Throughout the 1980s, Poland's economy continued to deteriorate. More and more Poles believed Communism had failed them, and they joined the Solidarity movement.

By the late 1980s, Poland's Communist leaders realized their days in power were numbered. They held talks with the leaders of Solidarity and other opposition groups. These talks led to an agreement allowing Solidarity to run candidates in the 1989 parliamentary election. The union won with a landslide. Its government was the first in the Soviet bloc since 1948 that was not Communist.

up through the ranks of the Hungarian Communist Party. By the end of the decade, their numbers were big enough, and their climbing had brought them high enough, that they could start making changes. The government initiated reforms in 1989 that led to approval of a multiparty political system (instead of a single-party Communist system), competitive elections, and the opening of Hungary's border with Austria.

The changes that happened in 1989 in Poland and Hungary had given hope to the East German people. Many had found their way out; others had found the courage to stay and demand change in their own country. It became harder and harder for the East German government to continue oppressing its citizens. Eventually, it became impossible, and the Berlin Wall came tumbling down. The wall had been the icon of Communism's hold on Eastern Europe. Once it fell, the other Communist regimes soon toppled.

After the Wall

Soon after the wall collapsed, Czechs and Slovaks staged street protests demanding political changes in Czechoslovakia. Dissident playwright Vaclav Havel led the demonstrations in Prague. Havel was

"You may ask what kind of republic I dream of. . . . I dream of a republic independent, free, and democratic, of a republic economically prosperous and yet socially just; in short, of a humane republic that serves the individual and that therefore holds the hope that the individual will serve it in turn. . . . The most distinguished of my predecessors opened his first speech with a quotation from the great Czech educator [Jan Amos] Komensky. Allow me to conclude my first speech with my own paraphrase of the same statement: People, your government has returned to you!"[2]

—Vaclav Havel, New Year's address to Czechoslovakia, January 1, 1990

cofounder of the reform group Charter 77. Thanks to Charter 77's maneuvering, the once-immovable Communist Party of Czechoslovakia transferred power to Havel and the reformers in December 1989. This transfer of power later became known as the Velvet Revolution.

In Romania, an armed protest by the Romanian people overthrew the Communist regime of hard-liner Nicolae Ceausescu also in December. Soon the Communist parties of Bulgaria and Albania also transferred power to reformers. European Communism was dying fast, including in Germany. In September 1990, the four Allied occupation powers and the two German governments reached an accord, called the Two Plus Four Agreement, that officially ended Germany's occupation. This allowed for German unification in

October 1990. These events effectively ended the situation in Germany created by World War II and the Potsdam negotiations.

Soon revolution spread to the Soviet Union itself. By 1990, the Ukraine and Baltic Republics (Latvia, Lithuania, and Estonia) had declared themselves to no longer be part of the Soviet Union. After surviving an overthrow attempt in 1991, Gorbachev was forced to transfer power to Boris Yeltsin. Yeltsin oversaw the dismantling of the Soviet Union. In 1991, Croatia and Slovenia declared independence from Yugoslavia.

Communism's collapse in Europe and the Soviet Union signaled the end of the Cold War. It ended the very real threat of global nuclear annihilation. It also brought

WAR IN THE BALKANS

Yugoslavia was a Communist state on the Balkan Peninsula, a finger of land that lies roughly between modern Italy and Turkey. It became Communist after World War II. It brought together Serbs, Croats, Bosnian Muslims, Albanians, Slovenes, and others in its federation. President Josip Broz Tito suppressed tensions among these groups.

Those tensions came back after Tito's death in 1980. Calls by nationalist groups for more self-rule within Yugoslavia led to Croatia and Slovenia declaring independence in 1991. Civil war and chaos broke out on the Balkan Peninsula. This violence lasted through the 1990s, resulting in the deaths of more than 140,000 people.[3]

REMNANTS OF THE WALL

Nearly 80 percent of the Berlin Wall is now gone.[4] Only a few physical reminders remain. On Bernauer Strasse, an observation tower still stands. Visitors can climb it and look down on a short stretch of preserved border strip. In the huge square at Potsdamer Platz, cobblestones trace the wall's route across the square and toward the Brandenburg Gate. On Niederkirchnerstrasse, 175 yards (160 m) of wall still stands, as does approximately 0.8 miles (1.3 km) of it on Warschauer Strasse. Checkpoint Charlie is now an array of shops and a small museum. In a cemetery northwest of town, a watchtower and a few wall fragments remain. Other traces remain too, but they are so small and hidden they are hard to spot without a guide.

sweeping economic change through globalization, the open trade of goods, capital, people, and ideas around the world.

But political freedom has not advanced as much as the economy during the past quarter-century. Since the 1990s, the governments of many states have continued oppressing their people. These have included members of the old Soviet bloc (such as Uzbekistan, Turkmenistan, and Russia), most of the Arab world, and Communist China and North Korea.

There's still work to be done. Only time will tell how much work it will take, and for how long, to bring to the world's people the freedom they dreamed of when the Berlin Wall came tumbling down.

Tourists view remnants of the Berlin Wall at Potsdamer Platz in Berlin.

TIMELINE

1945
The Soviet army wins the Battle of Berlin in May, ending World War II in Europe.

1945
Allied leaders meet at the Potsdam Conference from July 17 to August 2 and divide Germany and Berlin into four zones, each occupied by one Allied state.

1947
The United States proposes the Marshall Plan, which aims to aid war-ravaged European economies.

1948
East Berlin sets up its own city government in November, completing its separation from West Berlin.

1948–1949
The Berlin Blockade and the Berlin Airlift take place.

1949

On May 23, the Federal Republic of Germany (FDR) forms; the German Democratic Republic (GDR) forms on October 7.

1953

Workers in East Germany's cities go on strike June 16–17, and Soviet troops crack down harshly, killing several hundred people.

1960

East Germans flee the country to escape worsening conditions and ongoing harassment, restrictions, violence, and harsh demands.

1961

East Germany's government begins building the Berlin Wall on August 13.

1961

On October 25, US and Soviet tanks face off at Checkpoint Charlie.

1963

US President John F. Kennedy visits West Berlin on June 26 and delivers his famous "Ich Bin ein Berliner" speech.

TIMELINE

1971
Erich Honecker becomes the leader of East Germany.

1975
The Helsinki Accord is signed on August 1.

1976
East Germans start applying for exit visas, beginning
a movement that keeps growing until the wall falls.

1985
Mikhail Gorbachev comes to power in the Soviet Union.

1989
Hungary opens its border with Austria on May 2.

1989
The Communist Party falls from power
in Poland and Hungary.

1989

Hundreds of thousands of East Germans escape through the Austria-Hungary border from July to September.

1989

East Germany celebrates its fortieth anniversary on October 7.

1989

Massive protests break out in East Germany starting in October.

1989

On November 9, Günter Schabowski announces that East Germans may travel freely, effective immediately. Berliners overwhelm guards at the Berlin Wall, who open the checkpoints. The Berlin Wall falls.

1989

The Communist regimes of Czechoslovakia and Romania fall in December.

1990

East and West Germany reunify in October.

ESSENTIAL FACTS

Date of Event
1945–1989

Place of Event
Berlin, Germany

Key Players
- Harry Truman, president of the United States

- Winston Churchill, prime minister of the United Kingdom

- Joseph Stalin, dictator of the Soviet Union

- Erich Honecker, head of state of East Germany

- Mikhail Gorbachev, the president of the Soviet Union

- Egon Krenz, head of state of East Germany

- Günter Schabowski, party secretary of East Germany

Highlights of Event
- After World War II, Allied leaders divided Germany and Berlin into four zones, each occupied by one Allied country (France, the United Kingdom, the United States, and the Soviet Union).

- Tensions arose between the Soviet Union, a Communist country, and the United States, a capitalist country. These tensions are called the Cold War.

- From June 1948 to May 1949, Soviets blocked all land supply routes to West Berlin. The Western Allies survived by flying in supplies with the Berlin Airlift.

- East Germans fled to the West by the thousands in 1960 and 1961.

- On August 13, 1961, the East German government began building the Berlin Wall, preventing movement between East and West Berlin.

- On November 9, 1989, the Berlin Wall fell.

Quote

"Democracy is not perfect, but we have never had to put a wall up to keep our people in, to prevent them from leaving us. . . . While the wall is the most obvious and vivid demonstration of the failures of the Communist system . . . we take no satisfaction in it, for it is . . . an offense against humanity . . . dividing a people who wish to be joined together."—*US President John F. Kennedy, speaking in West Berlin on June 26, 1963*

GLOSSARY

archrival
One's main or most dangerous opponent.

bureaucratic
Relating to a system or organization that applies rules rigidly.

capitalism
A political-economic system in which business owners pay workers for their labor, but the business owners own the capital. The market determines the price of wages.

demilitarize
To remove or ban the presence of soldiers and weapons.

dissent
Political opposition to a government or its policies.

emigrant
A person who leaves his or her native country to live in another country.

exclave
A territory belonging to one country that is completely surrounded by the territory of another country.

fascist
Of or relating to a political ideology that favors leadership by a single dictator, central control of the economy, no tolerance for opposition, and extreme nationalism.

hippie
A person who rejects typical social views, favors peaceful living, and dresses in a style that includes long hair and beaded necklaces; became popular in the 1960s.

imperialism
The attempt of one state to control another.

infrastructure
Large-scale public structures, systems, and services that enable economic activity, such as roads, bridges, power supply, water supply, public transportation, and schools.

parliament
A state's legislature, usually made up of elected representatives.

propaganda
Biased information meant to further a cause.

punk
A person who likes the loud, fast rock music that became popular in the 1970s and who dresses in a punk style, typically with colored, spiky hair and clothing with safety pins.

regime
A particular government, especially an oppressive one.

ADDITIONAL RESOURCES

Selected Bibliography

Kempe, Frederick. *Berlin 1961: Kennedy, Khrushchev, and the Most Dangerous Place on Earth.* New York: Putnam's, 2011. Print.

Meyer, Michael. *The Year That Changed the World: The Untold Story behind the Fall of the Berlin Wall.* New York: Scribner, 2009. Print.

Senate Chancellery. "The Berlin Wall." *Berlin.de.* n.d. Web. 28 Jun. 2013.

Taylor, Frederick. *The Berlin Wall: A World Divided, 1961–1989.* New York: HarperCollins, 2006. Print.

Further Readings

Hay, Jeff. *The Fall of the Berlin Wall.* Farmington Hills, MI: Greenhaven, 2009. Print.

Hensel, Jana. *After the Wall: Confessions from an East German Childhood and the Life That Came Next.* Philadelphia: Perseus, 2004. Print.

Schmemann, Serge. *When the Wall Came Down: The Berlin Wall And The Fall Of Soviet Communism.* Boston: Kingfisher, 2006. Print.

Web Sites

To learn more about the Berlin Wall, visit ABDO Publishing Company online at **www.abdopublishing.com**. Web sites about the Berlin Wall are featured on our Book Links page. These links are routinely monitored and updated to provide the most current information available.

Places to Visit

Checkpoint Charlie Museum
Friedrichstrasse 43-45
D-10969 Berlin-Kreuzberg, Germany
49-0-30-25-37-25-0
http://www.mauermuseum.de
This museum is located next to the original Checkpoint Charlie border crossing in Berlin, Germany. It has permanent exhibitions about the Berlin Wall and East Germany. It also houses an exhibition focused on human rights around the world.

The Cold War Museum
PO Box 861526
Vint Hill, VA 20187
540-341-2008
http://www.coldwar.org
This museum contains both online and physical exhibits about the Cold War and the Berlin Wall. See artwork and read stories that tell visitors about personal experiences during this time in history.

SOURCE NOTES

Chapter 1. Escape from East Berlin

1. "Berlin Wall: Twenty Years after the Fall of the Wall One Man Relives the Last Escape from Checkpoint Charlie." *Mirror.* Mirror Online, 2 Nov. 2009. Web. 1 July 2013.

2. Ibid.

3. Ibid.

4. "The '80s: The Decade That Made Us: Escape from East Berlin." *National Geographic Channel.* National Geographic Society, 2013. Web. 1 July 2013.

5. Ibid.

6. Ibid.

Chapter 2. Postwar Berlin

1. Tilman Remme. "The Battle for Berlin in World War II." *BBC History.* BBC, 10 Mar. 2011. Web. 8 July 2013.

2. Ibid.

3. "Prelude to the Cold War." *PBS.* PBS, n.d. Web. 9 July 2013.

4. Frederick Taylor. *The Berlin Wall: A World Divided, 1961–1989.* New York: HarperCollins, 2006. Print. 52.

5. Ibid. 54.

6. Ibid. 46.

7. Ibid.57.

Chapter 3. A State Divided

1. Frederick Taylor. *The Berlin Wall: A World Divided, 1961–1989.* New York: HarperCollins, 2006. Print. 89.

2. "Before the Berlin Wall." *The Berlin Wall.* Newseum, 2013. Web. 10 July 2013.

3. Ibid.

4. Frederick Taylor. *The Berlin Wall: A World Divided, 1961–1989.* New York: HarperCollins, 2006. Print. 126.

5. Ibid. 155.

6. Ibid. 161.

7. "Two Sides, One Story." *The Berlin Wall.* Newseum, 2013. Web. 14 July 2013.

Chapter 4. Wall of Shame

1. Frederick Taylor. *The Berlin Wall: A World Divided, 1961–1989.* New York: HarperCollins, 2006. Print. 189.

2. "The Border Fortifications in the Eighties." *Berlin Wall Memorial.* Berlin Wall Memorial, 2013. Web. 14 July 2013.

3. Frederick Taylor. *The Berlin Wall: A World Divided, 1961–1989.* New York: HarperCollins, 2006. Print. 365.

4. Frederick Kempe. *Berlin 1961: Kennedy, Khrushchev, and the Most Dangerous Place on Earth.* New York: Putnam, 2011. Print. 394.

5. Ibid. 368.

6. Ibid. 384.

Chapter 5. Life in West Berlin

1. John F. Kennedy. "Remarks at the Rudolph Wilde Platz, Berlin." *John F. Kennedy Presidential Library and Museum.* John F. Kennedy Presidential Library and Museum, 26 June 1963. Web. 16 July 2013.

2. US Central Intelligence Agency Office of Current Intelligence. "Berlin Handbook." *Central Intelligence Agency.* Central Intelligence Agency, 27 Dec. 1961. Web. 16 July 2013.

3. Frederick Taylor. *The Berlin Wall: A World Divided, 1961–1989.* New York: HarperCollins, 2006. Print. 305.

Chapter 6. Life in East Berlin

1. US Central Intelligence Agency Office of Current Intelligence. "Berlin Handbook." *Central Intelligence Agency.* Central Intelligence Agency, 27 Dec. 1961. Web. 17 July 2013.

2. Frederick Taylor. *The Berlin Wall: A World Divided, 1961–1989.* New York: HarperCollins, 2006. Print. 373.

3. Carl Schoettler. "Samsung Moves into East Berlin." *Baltimore Sun.* Baltimore Sun, 20 Feb. 1993. Web. 17 July 2013.

4. Adolph N. Hofmann. "East Germany during the Wall." *Berlin and the Two Germanies, 1945–1989: From the End of WWII to the End of the Cold War.* n.p. Mar. 1990. Web. 17 July 2013.

5. Frederick Taylor. *The Berlin Wall: A World Divided, 1961–1989.* New York: HarperCollins, 2006. Print. 363.

6. John O. Koehler. *Stasi: The Untold Story of the East German Secret Police.* Boulder, CO: Westview Press, 1999. Print. 8.

7. Ibid.

8. Frederick Taylor. *The Berlin Wall: A World Divided, 1961–1989.* New York: HarperCollins, 2006. Print. 371.

SOURCE NOTES CONTINUED

Chapter 7. Changing Times

1. "Conference on Security and Cooperation in Europe: Final Act." *OSCE: Organization for Security and Cooperation in Europe.* OSCE, 1975. Web. 18 July 2013.

2. Erich Honecker. "Address by the First Secretary of the Central Committee of the Socialist Unity Party of the German Democratic Republic, Erich Honecker to the Third Stage of the Conference on Security and Co-operation in Europe, Helsinki, 30 July to 1 August 1975." *OSCE: Organization for Security and Cooperation in Europe.* OSCE, 1 Aug. 1975. Web. 18 July 2013.

3. Frederick Taylor. *The Berlin Wall: A World Divided, 1961–1989.* New York: HarperCollins, 2006. Print. 384–395.

4. Michael Meyer. *The Year That Changed the World: The Untold Story behind the Fall of the Berlin Wall.* New York: Scribner, 2009. Print. 68–69.

5. Frederick Taylor. *The Berlin Wall: A World Divided, 1961–1989.* New York: HarperCollins, 2006. Print. 401.

Chapter 8. The Fall of the Wall

1. Frederick Taylor. *The Berlin Wall: A World Divided, 1961–1989.* New York: HarperCollins, 2006. Print. 410–412.

2. Ibid.

3. Michael Meyer. *The Year That Changed the World: The Untold Story behind the Fall of the Berlin Wall.* New York: Scribner, 2009. Print. 159.

4. Ibid. 163–165.

5. "DOCUMENT No. 8 Günter Schabowski's Press Conference in the GDR International Press Center, 9 November 1989, 6:53–7:01 p.m." *Cold War International History Project Bulletin (Dec. 2013)*. The Woodrow Wilson International Center for Scholars, Dec. 2013. Web. 19 July 2013.

6. Ibid.

7. Michael Meyer. *The Year That Changed the World: The Untold Story behind the Fall of the Berlin Wall*. New York: Scribner, 2009. Print. 8.

8. Frederick Taylor. *The Berlin Wall: A World Divided, 1961–1989*. New York: HarperCollins, 2006. Print. 425.

9. Ibid. 426.

10. Michael Meyer. "Reporter's Notebook: The Story of a Lifetime." *Daily Beast*. Daily Beast, 21 Nov. 1999. Web. 20 July 2013.

Chapter 9. A Changing World

1. Glenn E. Curtis, ed. *Poland: A Country Study*. The Library of Congress, 1994. Web. 21 July 2013.

2. Vaclav Havel. "New Year's Address to the Nation." *Prague Castle*. Prague Castle, 1 Jan. 1990. Web. 21 July 2013.

3. "Transitional Justice in the Former Yugoslavia." *ICTJ*. International Center for Transitional Justice, 2013. Web. 21 July 2013.

4. "A Battle to Preserve the Berlin Wall as Cold War Landmark." *PBS Newshour*. MacNeil/Lehrer Productions, 8 Apr. 2013. Web. 21 July 2013.

INDEX

ABOUT THE AUTHOR

Christine Zuchora-Walske has been writing and editing books and articles for children, parents, and teachers for more than 20 years. Her author credits include books for children and young adults on science, history, and current events; books for adults on pregnancy and parenting; and more. Her book *Giant Octopuses* was an IRA Teacher's Choice book for 2001, and *Leaping Grasshoppers* was a 2001 NSTA/CBC Outstanding Science Trade Book for Students. Several of Zuchora-Walske's books have been well reviewed by *Horn Book* and *School Library Journal*. She lives in Minneapolis, Minnesota, with her husband and two children.

ABOUT THE CONSULTANT

A. James McAdams is the William M. Scholl Professor of International Affairs at the University of Notre Dame. He writes frequently about German politics and lived in both West Berlin and East Berlin before the fall of the Berlin Wall in 1989. McAdams is the author of *East Germany and Detente* and *Germany Divided*.